T0072494

50

SHADES

OF

IMPERFECT
IMPERFECTIONS

Shantise S. Funchest

Order this book online at www.trafford.com
or email orders@trafford.com

Most Trafford titles are also available at major online book retailers.

Print information available on the last page.

ISBN: 978-1-4907-8153-2 (sc)
ISBN: 978-1-4907-8152-5 (e)

Trafford rev. 04/17/2017

Trafford PUBLISHING® www.trafford.com
North America & international
toll-free: 1 888 232 4444 (USA & Canada)
fax: 812 355 4082

Acknowledgements

I would like to thank everyone who knows
me and knows my passion for writing
The ones who've been there for me and the ones who hasn't.
You all have given me strength to continue to do what I
love doing. No one is perfect. We all have flaws. Some of us
are battling our own demons, yet we still find the time and
strength to push forward, through the blood, sweat and tears.
It takes hard work. Nothing that comes easily is worth having!

YOU ARE RESPONSIBLE FOR
YOUR OWN HAPPINESS

LIFE IS WHAT YOU MAKE IT

50 Shades of Imperfect Imperfections

Also by Shantise S Funchest

Weak

They say what doesn't kill you, will eventually make you stronger,
But it's making me weaker,

I've cried several nights, even went days without sleeping or even
eating

As much as I treated you like shit, it never once crossed my mind
that you would be the one leaving

Guess you got fed up with all the drama I put you through, and
the suspicions of me cheating
Have you ever thought that I was only acting like that for a
reason?

We met through a mutual friend, and I felt like you were only in
my life for a season,
But as the time went by, I fell in love with you, even thou I was
the one who was actually cheating, on a man that I spent 8 years
of my life with.
Maybe that's my Karma, they always said she was a bitch

If I could learn from this experience and start all over I would, but
I wasn't shit when you met me just an open can of damaged goods
an individual misunderstood.

Maybe if I didn't treat you like all men were the same, I'll be somewhere living the happy life, maybe even rocking your last name.

Now I'm not going to put all the blame on me, you played your role in this as well.
Flirting, talking and texting different women like you were single.

Did you think I wouldn't be able to tell?
They say the same way you meet a person, is the same way you got to keep them.

You must've forgot how we met in the beginning, guess you can now call me the grand reaper.

It used to brighten up my day, when you were concerned and you would ask me "how was work?"

We'd have lunch together and talk about all the things that were going on or going wrong, but the communication slowed down and other people started grasping our attention son

Not to mention, the cyber world played a major role in this as well.

Yes, I stayed on social media Facebook and Instagram for hours at a time, because I wasn't getting that attention at home, how come you couldn't tell?

I know I bitched and I complained about me needing fresh air, but this wasn't the air I was referring to
None of this seems fair

How do you come home, don't say a word to me, you just pack up and leave?

You had all this planned out, what a fucked up way for me to grieve.

I guess I should stop crying rivers and start back eating
Seems like your minds made up at this point.
Well so is mine.
I promised myself I wouldn't want to get into anymore relationships.
Because I wouldn't want to waste someone else's time.

I don't blame you for your reaction to my actions, you were just being you.
Sorry I came into your life as a fuck up and all that I put you through.

I wish I could take the pain away, but it doesn't work like that.
Unfortunately, this is a reality and I've been hit with that reality check.

I could go on and on ranting about who was right and who was wrong, but what difference would it make if your already gone?

Awareness

I'm not afraid to admit I fucked up quite a few times
Taking you for granted, even wasting your time

I'm ready to change those fucked up ways, and it's hurting me
being without you for days

I don't know what I was thinking playing with your heart
I never gave you 100% from the start and that's what tore us apart

I never gave you a fair chance and I know it ain't right, but when
you love someone as much as I love you, you'll put up that fight.

Now I'm not ready for it to be all over with and I'll do what I
must do
To assure I don't want anyone else but you and that's the truth

Yeah my past relationships played a role in this too
Just because I was mistreated by different men all my life shouldn't
have affected you.

I was wrong more than I was right, and everything that happens
in the dark does come to the light.

I know you put your trust in me and I apologize
Despite my behavior and all my lies

But this apology is coming from deep down inside

I just want It to be us and no one else on the side

I'll admit to my dishonesty and my disloyalty to you, and yes I'll
change my ways
That's something I must do
Whether I'm with someone else or back with you

I know what I want, but I'll let you make that final call
If you have a change of heart and want to see other people I'm not
mad at all.

Fact

When you're so use to be mistreated by your past lovers
You can't tell the difference between a ruthless ass man
and a good brother

Every man that walk into your life you treat them wrong,
They put up with all they can deal with and eventually they leave
you alone.

Instead of giving yourself time to find you, and figure out what
you really want, you continue to search for Mr. Right even thou
your Mrs. Wrong

Now I'm not going to put all the blame on you,
but stop comparing these men to each other.
That's something you just got to do.

Soon as a man say that all women are the same
There go the bitch words and a long list of other names and mind
games

Every man you meet soon turns into your ex
Improperly getting to know who they are
Impatience is getting to you mentally and just like underwear
You move on to the next

You must think, is this what I want and where I want to be?
Only you can make those decisions only you, you see

Those decisions are something you must deal with and something you must live with

Flirting, calling, texting other men, not paying attention to the one who loves you, that's something you must chill with.

Focus your attention on someone who gives that same attention back, and again all men are not the same and that's a fact!

Transformation

Most of my smiles comes from hurt,
but I do whatever I must do, to make it work

outside of my home is where I transform
and without anyone watching i put that mask on

I walk around like I have the perfect life
Except when I return home at night
And all I do is cry

I know depression is a deadly disease,
but it's something I haven't mastered dealing with

Most of my fears come from being alone
And now that your gone,
I haven't felt comfortable being on my own

Most of this pain inside comes from the way I treated you
and now more than ever that's when I realize how much I needed
you

My heart was once filled with security
Now it's empty
Waiting on you to patiently return home
Baby I'm sorry, it was never you it was me,
and I was the one who was wrong

Let me love you

I know you heard the words I'm sorry all before
I know people walk in and out of your life, all the time
Well I'm willing to shut that door.

I just want someone who's going to love me for me,
and give me their all.
I'm talking about faithfulness, honesty and loyalty,
that's not asking for too much at all.

Someone who's going to cherish moment for moment and love me
unconditionally

Someone who's going to accept my flaws and work with me and
not give up on me

I'm not talking about sending me good morning text, but
Someone who's going to roll over and kiss me on the forehead and
tell me good morning instead.

I need someone I can dress up for and put on a show
Someone who I can share all my secrets with cause no one else
needs to know

Someone who makes me feel secure because I know he has my
back and the feelings are the same
Someone who eventually wants to get married one day and
wouldn't mind sharing his last name.

Someone who can admit and accept the fact that he may be wrong
Someone who doesn't party every weekend
And stay away from home

Someone who's grown enough to accept his responsibilities instead
of running away.
Someone who expresses his love and appreciation to me even
without saying it every day.

Someone who I can spend the rest of my life with, without
breaking the trust and be there for each other through thick and
thin.
That's the way it's supposed to be between a man and a woman
A wife and her husband!

Sincerely Apologetic

I'm sorry for a lot of things, but I'm not sorry for being introduced
to you, and giving you my heart,
but what I am sorry for plays one hell of a part,

I'm sorry for acting like I never care
Being selfish and treating you the way I did was completely unfair.

Having you come home to an uncooked meal
When you work your ass off, paying all the bills
Yeah that was a big deal.

I'm sorry for downing you, when as your woman I should've been
uplifting you
And supporting everything that you do,

But again, those selfish and inconsiderate ways got the best of me,
and I'm sorry for all that I put you through.

I'm sorry for not giving a fuck about your well-being,
and making you walk home at night

How inconsiderate of me when you're taking care of the household
like a man supposed to do and there's a car at home,
now that shit was dead wrong.

I'm sorry for going out into the world seeking attention from other
men

When I had a man at home who loved me to death
I just wasn't putting the time in.

I'm sorry for erasing all the text messages and the call logs off my
phone
It wasn't like I was sleeping with them so I didn't look at it as
being wrong.

I'm sorry for the lies, the dishonesty, the cheating and the flirting
Sorry for not taking your feelings into consideration to see that
you weren't complaining for nothing and you were hurting.

I'm sorry for not trusting you were different and not the same
Sorry for not returning the same love, I feel so ashamed.

Now I can apologize over and over until you become death to the
ears
Please know this apology is sincere, and these tears are real.

When you know better

If I knew what I know now, I would've done better
I would've treated you right and everything that you ever
complained about, would've been done without putting up a fight.

You were right, I had some fucked up ways,
and believe it or not I even had some fucked up days.

Me being the stubborn person that I am, I kept
all those feelings bottled up inside
That once pretty girl passenger is now riding on the driver's side.

I'm not afraid to admit I have flaws and I've broken a few hearts,
but I'm growing up now and I'm a better
person than I was from the start.

Perfect imperfection

Sorry I'm not perfect and I sometimes make mistakes
Sorry for being a selfish prick and always wanting things to go my way.

Sorry for being unfair and acting as if I don't care
Just the thought of my man with another woman is something I'm not willing to share.

Sorry for trying to play the role of the woman and the role of the man,
and not giving you a chance

Sorry for consistently apologizing for every time that I mess up instead of changing

Sorry for all the tears the headaches, the heartaches and the pain
Sometimes I wish that my eyes were wide open, but closed is that they remain

Sorry for thinking the grass was green on the other side
and when you gave me an inch, and let down your guard,
I took advantage and I let the wheels ride.

I thought you weren't paying me any attention, but I now realized
that you were and you were trying to see how much I loved you
and I let you hurt

I know you had certain expectations of me and I let you down
I shouldn't have never step down, and walked away from my
crown.

Unappreciated

Most times I feel as if I'm unimportant
No one will take me serious, because consistence does not exist
within me

Sometimes I feel unappreciated
One minute I'm loved by many
The next I'm hated by plenty.

To feel alone is the worse feeling to have
Those who you expected the most out of are the ones who are
quick to stab you in the back.

Well that's life and sometimes you must make the best of it
If you learn yourself, you become aware of who you are
You will figure out your place in life

Everyone may not deserve a place in your life and everything
happens for a reason

It's up to you to determine who stays in your life for good or for a
season.

It's okay to feel afraid of what is next to come
But if I were you I wouldn't or sit back and wait till it's my turn
You know the saying you don't know what you have until it's gone

Words hurt like Sticks and Stones

Whoever said, "words don't hurt" yes, they do
Especially if those words that were spoken were directed towards
you

It's only right to treat people how you want to be treated

Everyone has a sensitive heart and you'll never know until you
break it and the tables are turned

Don't say I never told you so, coming from an experience woman,
and a lesson learned.

A woman who was so used to treating people how she was being
treated
Instead of treating people how she wanted to be treated

and everyone who came into her life she ran them away not
realizing they were the ones that she needed.

Now that woman is lonely and her heart is cold, she never
imagined herself being as coldhearted as she was,

But the hole in her heart has left her hopeless and filled regret

Sometimes silence is better than speaking
For your words, can be as sharp as a knife and hurt someone
without physically touching them.

Wiser

Sorry for having you repeat yourself, when you use to tell me to stay in a child's place

Sorry for all the nagging and crying I did, when you'd tell me to give you some time and that you needed your space.

Sorry for acting out in class and making you leave work early just to come and pick me up

Knowing that you work your butt off to make ends meet and that your check would be cut short

Sorry for all the headaches I gave you
Sorry for being such bad luck.

Sorry for complaining when you'd tell me to do my chores before going outside

I should've known the type of person you are, you wouldn't let something like that slide

Be Fair

They say when you love someone, you just don't treat them bad
but that's usually what happens

you end up mistreating them
abusing them whether it's verbal, emotional or physical abuse

you end up belittling them and walking all over them like they're
the ground beneath you

when you're so use to being mistreated you don't know when a
good person comes into your life,

so, your mind is set on one thing, hurt them before they hurt you

not realizing that everyone is not the same

don't punish someone for someone else's mistake
don't blame someone for the pain caused by someone else

give everyone a fair chance for they just may be the one to open
your eyes and help you see what you've been missing

Read the chapter before you read the cover

Don't judge a book by it's cover
for everyone have a story to tell,
some are just more private than others

Just because someone is always smiling doesn't mean that their
heart isn't crying

We all live in our own demonic world where we're constantly
fighting demons everyday

So, when you judge someone without really getting to know them
How sway

Just because someone is always quiet
doesn't mean that they have nothing to say

We live in a world where no one really cares about your problems
and the struggles you face throughout the day

People put on a mask before they enter the real world
The mask hide their tears and most of all it hides their fears

It shields them from outsiders trespassing to their sanctuary
A place that's supposed to be sacred

A place where no one can read their minds and know what's going on inside
No one can hurt them no more than what they're already hurting

But when they're alone from the world that's when reality hits and the numbness fills their body and pains all over.
Demons reappear and haunt them

So, before you judge someone don't

Fed up

I met this chick who was down for me and in my corner through thick and thin
But all that didn't changed the fact I wasn't done playing in the sand

I let her down so many times
Coming home late,
Cheating with multiple women
Taking them out on dates

I got tired of all the nagging and clinginess
I couldn't take that shit

The constant cry's and whys
The questions start coming back to back like a heart attack

It wasn't the same in the beginning
Everything started to changed
Even after I gave his chick my last name
I still wasn't done playing games

Everything became a demand
And I never really got a chance to get to know her

One day I came home and the house was quiet. I expected dinner to be on the table like every night, even when I would come in late,

but this particular day there was no smell of food in the air.
Immediately I got upset cause she knew how I was.
Guess this day she didn't care

I went into the kitchen to find my wife's ring on the table on top
of a letter, she ended up leaving me and asking for a divorce.

She wouldn't answer any of my calls her phone continued to go
straight to voicemail
My text would read seen

I never wanted to hurt her, she would never understand
I was never meant to be a one woman's man

till this day, I live with regret cause I know I will never find
another woman like her

one thing I learned was to never take advantage of someone's heart
because when it backfires you may have lost everything

Too good to be true

The day you came into my life it has changed quite a big deal
I didn't take you seriously when you said you loved me
Everything was just too good to be real

I was blind to all the signs that you would give me, especially
when you would try to get me to realize that all men aren't the
same

I've been hurt so much I guess I never really let my guards down
I was only trying to protect my heart
It wasn't my intention to hurt you
And cause you so much pain

My new-found motto was to hurt them before they hurt you
They don't love you, you'll be just wasting your time
On a guy that has other women in his life

I couldn't afford to be that other woman, without putting on a
competition
Or fighting fire with fire

Not realizing that I was in control and I had all the power

No one has ever truly loved me or at least that's how it has felt

How can anyone love such a scorn woman?
Without her loving them back
And every time they bend over backwards she feels like she's being
attacked

How can any man see a heart that's dark and cold?
It's not perfect, but it would take a lot for you to mold

Take nothing for granted

Don't take my love for granted, for I've been hurt quite a few times
before
My mind is already weak and my heart is sore

I carry so more pain on my shoulder,
and you'd think maturity comes along with getting older

Age has no limitations to stupidity that corrupts the brain
And fills it up with poison
And blocks all air ways from getting fresh air

Heartaches have become the normal
And happiness used to be formal

But that's no longer into existence
For the damage is already done,
and every person that ever walked into her life instantly used her
as a pawn

she knew no better so she didn't know how to treat others
she was never given that woman to woman speech,
because she grew up without a mother

no woman role model in her life and no one she could trust
just like an old antique in the attic getting static and collecting
dust

so yes, she has trust issues and that's a fact
but how can you blame her when no one has ever loved her back?

Sometimes

Sometimes we repeatedly make the same mistakes over and over
until they become decisions that we chose to make

we may not look at it as being serious
until we actually see that person break

it doesn't mean that we don't have a conscious,
it doesn't mean that we are horrible people

some of us may need the proper guidance to move forward in life
some of us really are keepers

sometimes when someone good come along, we don't know how
to treat them right so, we treat them wrong

we hurt them unintentionally
we overlook their needs
and our needs have a lot to do with our freedom

we don't like to be suffocated, or given expectations
we just want someone who will overlook our flaws
and continue to be with us throughout it all

we're so used to being selfish and stubborn that they become an
option to our daily needs

We've been trapped in our own little world for so long

To when it comes to opening up
Even the ones who've been there for us through thick and thin are
wrong

Sometimes we make decisions that we later regret in life
Sometimes it takes from someone we love the most to walk out of
our lives

To help us realize that we really need to make a change
To let us know that things are no longer the same

A relationship is like canoeing
If you only have one paddle
You're not going to get that far
And if what's broken can't be fixed then the best thing for you to
do is to break apart

Inconsiderably wrong

I fell in love with a man whom I purposely knew was married
My married lover was everything I wanted in a man

I knew it wasn't right and I had to put myself in that woman's
shoes
So one day I called my married man,
and told him that there could no longer be an us.
For too long I been playing the role of a fool

He was upset with my decision, but he had to understand, that
I would no longer be a mistress to a married man

Vows aren't meant to be broken, and neither are hearts
I didn't want to be the reason why those two fall apart

Even thou I get a little aggressive and sometimes have an attitude
I still have a genuine heart
But I could no longer play the role of a fool

I had become the woman I always wanted to be
Discontinuing our affair was the beginning to a new start

I had to tell him if you really loved your wife,
and you have no intentions on leaving

Then why can't you be the man you're supposed to be
and stop cheating?

31

If the marriage is something you no longer want
Then maybe you should let her know

Don't fuck up something you love for something you like
I just thought I should let him know

One day I want to meet a man and I want to get married too
I wouldn't want him mistreating me the same way you mistreat
your wife

Yeah, I know we messed around quite a few time and I'll be the
first to admit it was inconsiderably wrong

If she's always there for you, when you need her, what would
happen if she's gone?

Appreciate what you have, don't go looking for what you want
Sometimes it may work out and sometimes it don't!

Runaway Boy

Even thou it hurts that your gone,
I know life must go on

But it will never be the same,
without you

How could I let you slip from in-between my fingers?
when I thought, I had such a tight grip on you?

This is all a surprise to me and I'm still not ready to unfold
Especially when both sides of the story have never been told.

You lead your friends to believe that I was doing you so wrong
So, they looked at me a certain way.

but you never took any type of recognition for the part that you
played

How could you go on in life, blaming everyone you encounter for
your wrong doings?
and just by you running away from your problems, just
who life do you think you screwing?

Are you going to be in different relationships all your life?
Not trying to settle down, not trying be a husband, make someone
your wife.

You're afraid to face your fears and take responsibility for your actions
It's just a small piece of the fraction

I knew you weren't perfect when I met you
But that was my choice to invest time into you

We could've built an empire together, could've been something great
Your so focused on you, and I know it's probably too late.

I hope one day you realize everyone's not out to get you, and life is what you make it.

Don't keep running away from your problems
Don't keep faking it

Wonder

Have you ever loved someone so much till it hurts to see them doing better without you?

To see the smile on their face, because they're with someone who accepts what your heart denied

Someone who was there to wipe their teary eyes
On the days you made them cry

Do it make you feel bad that you wouldn't provide a happier and healthier relationship with them?

Does it ever hurt to know that you took them for granted every opportunity that you had?

Now they've found true love and someone who invested in them instead

Flaws and All

Have you ever wondered what a relationship would be like, if both people were perfect?

No arguments and no fights
No one made mistakes, and no flaws

A wall built so strong that it wasn't capable of falling
Hearts so strong that it was impossible of breaking

No tears all smile
No gray hairs due to worries

Just perfection in two individuals who loved so strong
You did no wrong

Just perfection in two individuals who never cheated
Always remain faithful and loyal,
Respectful and honest

Have you ever imagined a relationship, where if both people didn't have anything nice to say?
The way to say it was to remain silent?

Starring at your soulmate communicating through their eyes

A relationship where two people go to bed not mad at each other,
for life is too short
To be anything other than happy

A relationship where you agreed to disagree

Well all relationships have flaws, that's right flaws and all!

Broken Vows

One day I woke up next to a woman I had met at the bar the night before, didn't even remember her name,

But the two of us lay naked under the sheets in her home, being a married man, I knew not going home to my wife was wrong.

That woman did things my wife wouldn't consider.
She wouldn't dare bring another woman into the home that we both shared,
Our sex life was dead and I don't think she cared.

I starred at the woman as she lay peacefully asleep
She was gorgeous, and single of course.

What would my wife think?
I knew the locks would be changed and I'm pretty sure she'll want a divorce.

I'm sure my clothes would be packed inside a suitcase
Sitting nicely on the curb waiting for me to pick them up

I was in no rush to go home, the dirt was already done,
and I wasn't ready for the outcome.

I'm not sure how the sex was the night before, but this time we made love
Neither one of us using protection

I prayed I didn't catch an infection or something worse, but she assured
me that she was clean and her occupation was a practical nurse.

Who can I blame? Only myself.

My phone rang, it was my wife

The sex was so good I let the call go straight to voicemail

By that time, I got a text message from my boy Rell.
letting me know she texted looking for me, asking was I in jail.

She knew I wasn't the type to spend nights out.
This woman had me after a couple of drinks, but I had to make
this quick
And get home to my wife I knew she was worried sick.

After I finish breaking her off
I knew I had to be on my way, o'l girl tried to get me to stay but I
wasn't going.
I knew what I had at home, but I wasn't done hoeing

Yes, men can be hoes as well, in reality we're all the same
We breathe the same air
We play the same games
If you going to judge a man and a woman, be fair

I got in my car and sped home on the E-way repeating the lie I
would tell her over and over in my mind
Once you tell the first lie, you had to continue lying

And of course, you had to remember the lie you originally told
Unless you want to keep it honest or shall I say bold?

I pulled up to my drive-way not too long after
There were no suitcase or clothes on the curb

I walked in the house and heard the shower water running.
So I tiptoed upstairs and by the time I got to the top of the stairs
there was my wife with a dry towel in her arms

I asked her was she getting in the shower
She replied "No but you are, I'm sure you stink, for whatever
reason you felt the need to stay out all night".

I told her I got locked up for fighting at the bar last night.
She looked at me and said "of course your right".

Just as I let out a silent sigh, she said, "Listen here, I tell you why".
"you see I always thought you were having an affair, but I didn't
have enough evidence to share"

So I hired a private investigator to follow you around town
To the market, barbershop, mailbox, even the kids school
I could no longer play the role of a fool

Lastnight brought me to reality and a clear vision
I don't want to hear no excuses, because you had a decision
But you did what you wanted to regardless of being a married man
Spending the night out sleeping with another woman

Did you think I was stupid enough to continue to accept this? But
of course my mind's made up and I'm asking for a divorce

Before you assume,
I won't put you out, or damage any of your personal possessions
But you're no longer welcome in the master bedroom
Therefore, you can make your transition to the guest room

I won't fight for the house you can have it all
The only thing I wanted was to be happy
That wasn't asking for too much at all

There are no elevators to success

You can't live in a world thinking everyone owes you something
You must work for what you want if it's really what you want

Nothing comes freely, but everyone's needy and always expect
handouts without a doubt.

It doesn't work like that. Successful people are the ones who
knows it takes hard work and dedication to get to the top
The people who knows the floor must be swept before it can be
mopped.

Something easily given, is nothing earned

Survival Guide

It's crazy how everything can go from sugar to shit in a blink of an eye
Feelings are no longer mutual and the love so easily to die

Smiles eventually turn into cries
Hello's soon become goodbyes
You constantly ask yourself why?
Why was everything so perfect in the beginning?
I'm not understanding what it means when they say everything has an ending

Is it of human nature to hurt and carry so much burden on one's shoulder?
The more mistakes that we make and loses that we take as we get older

Why can't everything we do in life be of accuracy,
and proven satisfactory?
Imperfect imperfection has become our greatest identity

Blood type not perfect is what runs through our veins
Isn't it insane?
To want the best out of life is yet to come
Life moves on an angle
No navigation to none

No guides on how to live, no role models to help you get through
the difficult times
No one to look out for one another these days
The street talks but the information is not sufficient
No one open their mouths when they know a person has done
wrong

Don't even show remorse when that person is no longer alive
Life is a just survival game without the remaining lives
and a survival guide

Flow

When you've been treated a certain way for
so long, you become used to it
Your expectations are at an all-time low

No self-respect nor self esteem
No raising the standards
You just go along with the flow

100%

If you're looking for perfect, I am not the right person for you
I have flaws, I make mistakes and bad decisions from time to time
I might be a dime,
but perfect does not define who I am
Overall I am a person who loves with all that is in me

A person who you can depend on in the time of need
That'll have your back
And pick up your slack
If you're fucking with me

A down ass chick for the right guy
I'll be your Bonnie, you be my Clyde
And we ride by each other side till the day we die

I like attention from my man and to be treated like a queen, while
I treat him like a king
You can't have two people and only one fighter in the ring

It takes participation from the both of you
To make it work and the get through,
whatever obstacles life may put you through

relationships aren't 50/50 it's a 100/100
why only put in half the effort and expect a different outcome

you can't rent an apartment and only pay half the rent

but these days' sense isn't common anymore
you get what you put into a relationship
and if you do that you just may get more

No settling

Afraid of being alone, so you settle for less
Not a day goes by that you don't stress
I'm not impress
But life is just a test

You'll never be happy until you are truly at a point where you
could convince yourself that you deserve better than what you've
been putting up with

You'll never find peace within until you let all the negativity go
You could be passing up on a blessing
But being with someone who doesn't make you happy just so you
can say you have someone you'll never know

Sometimes it's not always good to go with the flow
Turn around, go in the opposite direction
Don't be afraid of taking chances, just go!!

What do you have to lose? The same chance you'll take to win.
To love someone, you must first learn to love within
Yes, love yourself get you some counseling
Some sort of help

Yeah life throws you balls, but you must learn defense and give it your best shot

Again, life is what you make it and you're just over-exaggerating about it being that bad cause it's really not.

Winners Don't Lose and Losers Don't Win

There's always someone out there who'll
give anything to take your place
So, don't think that you're going through
so much that it's too much to bare

To you, life may not be fair, but that's not true at all
Sometimes you'll trip and sometimes you'll fall

Get back up and try again
It may take a few tries, but eventually you'll win.

Beautiful Creature

Regardless how crazy I may seem
I'm only crazy for you

No matter how upset I am
It may be because of you

I regret nothing
I appreciate everything that you do

So, let me have my moment
Because every girl needs one too

And every girl needs private time
Where she can wine, and dine
And clear her mind

Were just beautiful creatures
Who just want to be loved and spoiled
and not have the feeling that were wasting our time

we don't want to have the feeling that we are giving more than
what we're receiving

when we could actually be focusing on our goals
and achieving

we like to be heard, sometimes with no advice needed
just a listening ear
to listen to our spoken words
and a shoulder to lean on when we need it

we like to be held and told everything will be alright
we'll fight and we'll fuss before we give up and leave
women are more patient than men
for you 'all it just takes one time
for us to do wrong and yawl throw that in our face for a life time

Single Woman's Prayer

Send me a man that's faithful and only have eyes for me
One who'll love, respect and cherish me
Let him be loyal, honest and everything I need him to be
Please send me a man one who's only for me

Let him be a rider and a provider
And a coach when I'm of my game

Let him be marriage material
Someone who won't make me regret taking their last name

Let him be handsome, well groomed
And smelling good

I deserve someone of my preference
Every woman should

Please let him be worth my time
It's something I can never get back

Let the sex be A-1
I am not settling for whack

Someone who'll be my protection
And have my back

Let him be a listening ear
Whether I'm right or I'm wrong

Send me my dream man
I've already been waiting too long

Realize Reality

When your man comes home from a long day's work
Be considerate, have dinner made
Don't be suck a jerk

Have the shower ran when he's pulling up in the drive way
Give him a massage
Just be his peace
Don't get in the way

Don't make him put in all the work
When he's busting his ass all week

The last thing he want to do is come home,
arguing and fighting with his girl
When he's already out there fighting one against the world

Our black men already hard it hard enough
Nagging and complaining all day everyday
Honey slow down you're doing too much

Everything doesn't have to be an argument or fight

Sit down take a deep breath talk about it
Two wrongs don't make a right

If he's doing you wrong and you keep allowing it
Then what are you complaining about obviously you like that shit

To be an Option, is not an Option

Never second guess yourself,
you were right the first time

Never be someone's option,
priorities are always first in line

You could be doing something beneficial with your time
Instead, you're out searching for rings without diamonds
Looking for mountains to climb

Love can't be forced
It's always unexpected

You teach people how you want to be treated,
and that's well respected

If the other person isn't treating you right,
And you've never been on a plane before it's time for you to take
your first flight

No one deserves to be mistreated by someone that they love
And no one should ever allow them to

Shantise S. Funchest

There's someone for everyone out there
You just have to find that matching shoe

When you find that shoe, you tie them strings tight
Loose shoestrings will have you slipping and tripping
Loosing either one or the other, Mr. or Mrs. right

You choose your life

I did some things I shouldn't have done in my life-time
Which I knew it was wrong
But I was just a teenager back then and I was only having fun

I grew up a lot from that lifestyle of running wild and parted my
ways,
and I must say I grew up to be better than okay

I'm kind of glad it turned out the way that it did
And I left that street life alone before it got serious

Some of us make it and some of us don't
You have an option to make

Child Killer

I am not about that street life never was never been
But it's crazy growing up in the chi
Cause the only people who are dying are all the children

Have you ever wondered what those children could of became as
they got older?

Future lawyers, doctors, nurse and teachers
An all-star player waiting to play sitting on the bleachers

Do you ever think how their family deals with their absence on a
daily?
How would you feel if it was one of your own your brother, sister
or even your baby?

Are your conscious so numb till you just don't give a fuck?
I hope they place you in general population and let those other
inmates fuck you up

You're a coward, who doesn't have a conscious you're ruthless and
a disgrace
And on this earth, you don't deserve to have a place

I'll be glad when Illinois come up with a death penalty
I'll surely support it
Without a doubt

No exceptions to the rule
You kill a child and that's light out

The people who pretend to be so hurt and so shooked are prabably
the same mf's putting money on those killer books.

Loyalty

Get you someone who's going to stick by your side through the up's and the down's

Loyalty is hard to find these days
Something like that doesn't easily come around

Recognize the real from the fake
The love from the hate,
And the decisions from the mistakes

If a person truly love you, they'll do whatever it takes
just to keep you

To protect you
To be there in the time of need

They're pride won't let them turn their back on you
No matter the situation
And money won't turn into greed

Find someone you can invest in and that'll do the same thing for you
Find you someone who keeps you smiling with everything that they do

Potential

We live in a world where we say "Be careful"
Instead of see you later

Funerals have become family reunions

Being beautiful has become, being a bad bitch
And if you beat the PA system you were considered living rich

We live in a world,
Where no one is satisfied with the way they were born, and you
can't tell the difference between girl and boy

Respecting our elders, no longer exist
And the board of education don't give a damn how many days of
school a child miss

We live in a world where more schools and libraries are closing
And more prisons are unfolding

Waiting for the youth to fail
Like it's always been
But change can't start outside
It starts within

Home is the first place where a child should learn
But these days you have parents who's strung out on drugs, locked
up and running the streets

Like the saying that's true a apples don't fall far from the tree

It doesn't have to be your child you can always be a child's mentor
and lead them in the right path
Believe it or not every child has some sort of potential

When the beat drops

He came into my life and tried to love me
But I pushed him away

The past had caused so much hurt, and I had built a wall so strong
That I couldn't believe anyone was capable of loving me

He fulfilled my needs gave me anything and did anything I asked
him to do
But who was going to love me, after all that I had been through?

My trust in men had disappeared throughout the years
That I feared to open up to anyone still came my way

But this man was strong enough to tear down that wall
Without letting me fall

I gave him a chance, but I didn't give my all

I never gave it my all, my pride wouldn't let me
It covered my heart like a shield, it wouldn't let no one neglect me

Maybe I should've put my trust in him,
put more effort into what we had
I never meant for it to end like it did

Crazy how I missed my beat
When and if another opportunity presents itself
I promise i'll be quick on my feet

Granted

Missing you has become a part of my daily routine
I never expected you to have such an impact on my life

Even thou we fuss and we fight
I always thought we were tight
at least make things right

Guess I wasn't right this time
It affects me now more than ever before

The events repeatedly play over and over in my head
Of when you walked out that door

I'm nowhere near perfect and I think you should give me a second
chance
As I would give you
I'm taking full responsibility for my actions, no one else is to
blame

I can't even fake loving you.
If I ever told you I didn't, I was telling a major lie
I never wanted you to catch feelings for me
Because I knew eventually I'll hurt you

I never knew what it felt like to love someone, but I fell deeply in
love with you
Regardless of what we've been through
I had no intentions on leaving you

When you proposed that night it left me numb
It wasn't the first time someone had proposed to me and left me
alone

So, I took it how I always took things and I chopped it up as a loss
before it even became a lost
I just got tired of playing games with men and getting my hopes
up high
Only for them to be selling me a lie

Please forgive me I'm ready to settle down now and the games are
gone out the door

I will no longer take your love for granted I promise not anymore

Split personality

She had several personalities, one for each day of the week
She was bored with being just one person, so to speak

She figured if she changed who she was each day
that no one could get in her way

Although she had a different color wig
To match her everyday outfit

Her love life was a mess and not only that she had a person for
everything that she needed,

Because one person couldn't do it all, so she put each one to the
test

From a chauffeur to a maid, a butler, bar tender, chef, personal
trainer and masseuse

You name it she had it all
One to do everything that only one could not do

She was never a simple girl
She had to keep her life exciting with everything that she did

And you couldn't tell her nothing from the sheets to the bed

She lived a boring life when she was only one person and people
would take advantage of her

But when she became multiple personalities she was a force to be
reckoning with

No one could provoke her ego,
Because her personality was split

Conscious

You ever heard the saying "there's a stranger in my bed?"
Well let me tell you about this

One afternoon of getting in from work
I done like I usually do

And that's fix a cup of herbal tea
And something slight to eat.

Well I done just that and I've gotten a little light headed
So, I decided to get in the bed

As I got closer to my master bedroom
I could feel the energy being drained from my body

It was like a force of some sort weighing me down

By the time, I made it to my resting place
There was a figure lying there instead

Now I know I set the house alarm, how could anyone get into my
home
There were no signs of a break in,
But the intruder was there plain as day

And this person was laying in my bed underneath my covers

I stare at the figure only to realize we kinda resemble,
and the features were like no other
"who are you?'
How did you get into my home?
Why are you here?

The figure starred at me and said
"is that really a question you must ask my dear?"

I'm not understanding the reason of your presence, what do you
want from me?

"I don't want anything from you"
I am your conscious.
You my dear have awaken on the wrong side of the bed and left
behind something of value

Notice how grumpy you've been throughout the day
How defensive you've been when you thought someone would get
in your way

How you've worked by yourself
Try not to leave me at home, if not taking daily I'm dangerous to
your health

Missing

I forgot what's it's like to have a normal sleeping pattern
Late nights when I should be sleeping
That's when my mind wonders, isn't that creepy?

It's like a scratched cd of if's, why's, how's, when's and where's
No answer's just questions followed by a blank stare

I wish I had answers to my questions, but
Unfortunately, I don't

Even my mind knows that and you'll think it'll let me sleep
peacefully
But it won't

I've tried talking to my pillow, but it's tired of the disturbance
It just sits back and continue with the observance

Decisions

In life, you'll come across decisions that will either move you
forward or push you back

But the decision is all yours, whether you want to be back on track

That's life for you. To some it doesn't come easily,
But at the same time, it's what you make out of it.

You find yourself either climbing mountains or jumping over
puddles
Just to live up to others expectations
Not being honest and putting yourself in awkward situations

You must love yourself before you can love anyone else
Or it will never be right and you must have patience with the
decisions that you make
and the paths that you take

remember no one can step in your shoes and take your place
that doesn't mean you give up and leave a vacant space

Support

Isn't it funny how people are so quick to support celebrities and
people that they don't know,

Rather than supporting someone they knew for years,
Crazy that's the way life go

That's when you know jealously and envy takes over and it kills
them to see anyone who was once on their level
or beneath doing better

I don't envy anyone I want us all to be successful and make it
I'm so real that I can't even fake it,
but the way we treat each other I swear I hate it

I was always the type who wanted to lend a helping hand to
anyone who wanted to help themselves

But at the same time, I can't stop what I'm doing and
put my priorities on the shelf

Living is sinning

No one is perfect, we live to sin
Whether it's having a child out of wedlock
Wearing fake nails, eyelashes, phony hair, anything for us to fit in

Whether we're partying 6 days out of the week
At church on Sunday's
Who are you to judge in what way someone sin?

Doesn't matter if we turn gay or lesbian
We'll still be judged, by whoever it may offend
Because we don't fit in

Cheating while being married is also considered a sin
There's a thousand ways to define how one may sin,
but who are you to judge that's your own personal opinion

Built Strong

They called me ugly, stupid and blind
I wasn't popular in school and I had no friends,
but I knew I'll be just fine

They stole from me
Curse me out and called me names.
I didn't let words hurt me and knock me up off my game

They tore up my finish work, all because I had straight A's
Tried to humiliate me in any way
But that still didn't change how I went about my day

One day they stop and tried to be my friend
They saw I wasn't giving in
and no matter how hard they tried, the shoe was now on the other
foot and they tried so hard to fit in

Compatible

Hold me down and never give up on me
I'm just an imperfect individual who wants to be treated like I
matter to someone

I want to receive the good morning text
someone telling me they love me
asking how my day is going

I want those candle light dinners
Those random kissing on the cheeks

I want someone to overlook my flaws and forgive me for my
mistakes
Someone who I can build something with
A business partner, someone who I can deal with

Someone who's just about tired of getting it wrong and want to get
it right like me
Someone who's compatible with me and won't give up so easily

The Wrong type of Attention

Never understood why women seek validation
From others

They become social media whores, who thrive off attention
Not to mention

The number of likes pump their heads up and they can't recognize
a man that's truly interested

They think every man that comes their way only wants to get in
between their legs
and they try to escape that type of attention

So use to being with men who pop them off and leave them to
take care of their kids on their own
Can you blame all the men who's in your inbox on daily?
Maybe If you've never gave them that type of reason they wouldn't
be in there just maybe

Agree to disagree

Agreeing with someone doesn't necessarily mean that they're always right
It means that you have no energy to argue the fact that they may not be

Just because you agree with them doesn't make you vulnerable or weak
It just means that you know when and when not to speak

It may be best at times,
may save you from the worse that ever may come your way,
But it's ok just let it be

And that's what it means when they say you have to agree to disagree

If the crayon is blue and to them it's red
Don't agrue the fact that they may be colorblind
Something your eyes can not see
Another example or agreeing to disagree

If it's raining and they think it's snow
Don't waste your time arguing that's it's not
Just go along with the flow

Past Mistakes

The mistake we make is when we dig up our past
When we're in a relationship with someone else

We compare the two together instead of learning and moving
forth

We focus on what we're so use to, instead of what could be
Not giving that person a chance to show us something other

Afraid of commitment, because we find ourselves in the same
situation over again
Not understanding that happiness starts within

How can we be happy if the past is weighing us down, affecting
our present and destroying our future?

There's nothing no one can do to make us happy, if we keep
holding on to something that once came to an end

If you keep holding on to the past everything that you begin will
soon come to an end

Creeping

You got a man at home, but you're creeping
What's the reason you won't leave him,
Is it because he's also cheating?

Do you love him?
Is it because of financial stability

Because you don't have the ability to leave
To stand on your feet

You've been spoiled for so long
That you accept however he treats you and does you wrong

Spend nights' out
Text messages and incoming calls coming in all night long

You don't speak of it in fear he'll leave you with nothing
Too scared to confront him
To demand what you want and how you want to be treated

Yet you sit back and accept all that is thrown your way and you
stay heated
And once again you've proven that you
Have become defeated

Creeping doesn't make the situation better
It just proves that you rather play the game instead of demanding respect

Something that all woman should want from a man
Especially their man

"Never let your man make you #2 to no woman"

Grown Men's Shoes

I really despise men who pretend that they're in love, but it's the financial dependability from the woman that put up with their stuff

Whatever happened to men being the sole providers and head of households?
The way the world is today, the roles are turned. Here's something you should know.

More and more women are finding the strength and standing tall
While more men are sitting back waiting on a come up or a blessing to fall

Be the man that a woman needs, not a man that needs a woman
We're already raising children of our own
You were your own responsibility once you became grown
If I work, you better have a job as well
If you're a sales person, you better make that sell
I will not stand for anything and I mean anything at all
I was taught to get out and get it on my own
Nothing came to me so easily, nothing that I can recall

Yeah men look at me because I'm gor geous, but hey they miss the important part
Anyone can look this good, but are they intelligent? Do they have goals they want to accomplish? I mean after a couple dates, what's next?

Can they hold an intellectual conversation without it leading to sex?

See when I put my time and effort into something I give it my best
I not investing time into an overgrown man, who don't have anything going for himself,
Not a skillet to cook food in or insurance for his health

Relationships are supposed to be equal and we do for each other
I'm your woman and That's something that's totally different from being your mother

I didn't raise you or bathe you I'm not type of chick
I don't care if the dick is good and you give good head

So, when you look at me, just know one thing
I'm not lowering my standards for no man, and this isn't what it seems
Be a real man and do what real men do
Stop depending on a woman and step in a real man's shoe

Blind-Sided

She looked for love in all the wrong places
So many men fell in love with her exterior, that she couldn't match
names to faces
The vulnerability and greed exceeds her needs and the many men
that she tries to leave

The stalking and the obsession
she have to deal with on a daily still didn't show her a lesson
just one day maybe,
maybe one day she'll come to her senses and understand that men
are going to be men
no matter what, maybe one day she'll stop with all the impressing

life could be a wonderful test
it's like an Act or Sat you know the one where we try to do our
best

you might flunk at it and fail quite a few times, but the worse of it
all when you don't get back up after the fall.

LIFE IS WHAT YOU MAKE IT

We were born to be

Kings and Queens

No one is born perfect and everyone makes mistakes. You can't change someone to fit your expectations. It is he himself who wants to be a better person. Trust is earned, respect is given, loyalty is everything and love is ghost. no one plans to fall in love, but if you have someone who's there for you and continuously prove their love, don't pick up stones in search of diamonds!

Printed in the United States
By Bookmasters